If The World Is Running Out
Poems by Kate Green

Ilene Alexander

# If The World Is Running Out

Poems by
Kate Green

Introduction by
Patricia Hampl

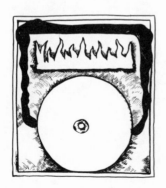

Holy Cow! Press • MINNEAPOLIS • 1983

Grateful acknowledgment is made to the editors of the following publications in which some of these poems first appeared: *A View from the Loft, Ironwood, Milkweed Chronicle, Sing Heavenly Muse!,* and *Twin Cities Magazine.* "Things A Woman Does With Emptiness" originally appeared in *A Change in Weather: Midwest Women Poets,* edited by Peg Lauber (Rhiannon Press).

*I would like to thank Molly LaBerge, Executive Director of COMPAS' Minnesota Writers In The Schools Program, for her many years of encouragement and support.*

ISBN 0-930100-15-8

Library of Congress Number: 83-080592

Photograph of Kate Green by Timothy Francisco

Cover drawing and all drawings © 1983 by Ellen Kennedy Goodell

First Printing

Typesetting by Annie Graham & Co., Iowa City, Iowa

Printed in the United States of America

**Publisher's Address:**

Holy Cow! Press
Post Office Box 618
Minneapolis, Minnesota 55440

**Principal Distributor:**

Bookslinger
213 East 4th Street
Saint Paul, Minnesota 55101

*For Burton Looney*

# TABLE OF CONTENTS

# INTRODUCTION

*It was nothing, it was important . . .*

This efficient paradox (the first line of "Zero at the Center") is poised over the conundrum of poetry — not only Kate Green's poetry but poetry, period. This conundrum is a riveting mystery, and maybe can be described in this way: While life is a series of unevenly spaced flashes (of despair, joy, boredom, awe — you name the moods) and nothing makes sense for long, the poet must chart this — well, this mess, and must make of it not simply sense but music. As the poem goes on to say, we must "begin with nothing like God."

The materials of true poetry are always humble, absolutely idiosyncratic, the autobiographical tatters that, in gifted hands, are made into the memoir that fits us all. That is, poetry is the sung voice of accurate perception. "I want to show you this world," Kate Green says in the title poem. This is the statement of a real poet.

It is also the statement of a mother — the poem is addressed to her infant son. But this child is going to have a very interesting time of it — as will readers of this book — because this mother, this poet, means it: the world presents itself as a gorgeous, dangerous place and the view is from a bridge over a freeway slashing through her neighborhood where

> we ride behind glass, hands clenched to wheels,
> radio tuned to jazz to soothe
> the cramped and hurried spine.
>
>           — "If the World Is Running Out"

Readers of Kate Green's earlier work will be looking, perhaps, for a more sensuous landscape. And the body is still lusciously here in these new poems. An even wiser body, sinuous as well as sensuous. There's no need to ask the body, or poetry — or the big bad world — to be pretty in order for it to be infinitely fascinating. The profound commitment of love reveals itself in sex and in attention to the world:

> Live out your ecstasy on earth
> amid the flaking patio stones,

*the boarded-up back door*
*and the rusty car.*

— "Don't Make Your Life Too Beautiful"

It's hard to say what has prompted the easy but certain authority of these poems, the exactitude of the images, the range of concerns, the wisdom and relish of the humor, the acquiescence to the past. Whatever has empowered her, Kate Green has found not simply "a voice," as the saying usually goes, but an ear for the voices of others who would sing. And can she sing.

There are stunning portraits here — Estalee, her black mother-in-law contending with this white poet daughter-in-law; Blanche, the poet's grandmother hanging on to the dignity there is in accurate memory; Jim White, a friend who dies.

The prose poems and some of the longer portrait poems that rely on dialogue approach fiction. Or rather, they are fully successful stories, sometimes (as in "Baptism") told in the wonderfully realized voice of another person.

But the notion of narration, of stories being told, goes deeper in this collection than the distinction between narrative and lyric poetry. There is the sense here — and maybe this is where part of the authority of the poems comes from — that we must tell our stories to each other . . . or beware.

The world is full of mystery but it must not be choked with secrets: we must talk to one another. From the private heart, from neighbor to neighbor, from past to future, parent to child and back again, from race to race, class to class, sex to sex. Amazingly, Kate Green has poems in this collection which do each of these things. She ranges all over the social fabric, knowing the voices of white and black, people working the night shift in the factory, people who "have careers," as Estalee says.

Lots of stories that make good reading in this book. Lots of beautifully written lines — but nothing ever for beauty alone, as the last poem in the book instructs. The luxuriant sensuality of Kate Green's earlier work has found its home and its vocation in this new, powerful collection of poems, knowing that

*We make ourselves up as we go,*
*making love up as we dream,*
*and wake to touch what we've made.*

— "Possible Love, Possible Sky"

These poems are tactile and immediate, rhythmically charged. They are also thoughtful, political in the inevitable acknowledgment of relation. They are remorseless with observed moments, snatches of spoken conversation—but they are never bitter or crabby. Everything here is honest, respectful. The relish of the body has matured into a deep commitment to "the daily years."

Like anything truly beautiful, this book seems not beautiful but necessary. For if the world *is* running out, this book is full of the cries we must make, the songs we must sing.

— *Patricia Hampl*

"Every poem is meant to be a story."
— *Cesare Pavese*

I.

## LABOR DAY

Early September night, my father and mother
sit on the porch, fan mosquitos off,
drink the clear and lonely glasses —
Yellow: beer.
Luna green: gimlet.
Bluing in reddish light: sky over lake.
Dark hums them with Ella Fitzgerald on the hi-fi.
I sit on damp black sand near smell of seaweed
burying an ant over and over.
I don't know the song but it comes in me.
Gnats cloud above in a swarm.
*Savoy the home of sweet romance,*
*Savoy will win you at a glance.*
Mother has dyed her hair red for the summer.
Father drives up north on Friday afternoon
and the drinking starts.
Seaweed floats in. Old logs crumble at the shore.
The ant crawls out. Ella sings,
*You gave her your heart too*
*Just like I gave mine to you*
*And you broke it in little pieces*
*Now how do you do?*
All in my reach, milkweed swollen warty
will burst in a few weeks,
pile of broken shells I collected
then stepped on.
Ant exhausted in sand.
Above me, voices clink in sweet ice glasses.
Summer dark crawls up out of the slough.
First, a chill off the lake,
then a great blue heron rises
slow as the hot moon from the shadows,
wings outspread
like a cross the sky is nailed to,
flopping gracefully out
over the empty water.

## MOTHERBODY

When I used to go bare-nippled into summer
on a day the light stayed late to love us,
my mother and I slid naked from dusk
into the lake

The water drank her thighs
I watched her sink,
the water-skin surround her
woman-hair and belly,
brown nipple islands,
round of breasts and shoulders,
wind of her evening hair

And wanting my body to become her
I feared to become her,
to swell open like her,
a wave breaking into womanskin

What of that scar
stitched to her white belly,
I saw,
I saw in the luminous blue —
what death did that sew up?

What of the tumorous growth
of my own breasts?
At night I would touch them
as if they were a cancer

Wanting to bleed like I heard,
like I heard

And feeling the hair
down the curve of my pubic stone,
feared the first black hair that sprang from me
*I am growing back to an animal*

When I fingered my womb's lips for the first time
I felt I would fall into myself forever,
swirl in the blood maze of my body

to crimes so dark
no one would even name them

How could I learn myself?
I watched her,
watched her
Stole her body into my own

Daughter, circling
out of her cells
Daughter, the call she sent
into the waving instant

Gnats whined over us
A loon split the distance with her call
My mother dove under
and held the water pulse
till the ache to breathe was too much
and she rose like a white stone
lifting out of the water

Deep in me I hear our body
where I sunk out first roots
in her liquid pulse,
where my pure brain
hummed in her
learning the music
inside the names for things

SUNBATHING

Breasts of the sky
and absence
Blue hair
piled on earth
Cumulous sky-flesh
and the ancient spring

In the pale heat
I touch my nipple
Its roots
sink to my womb
Your circling fingers,
how they burned in me,
making up skin
as a movement of tongue,
language of wind cry,
wave written in flesh

My petals open
to a black hot center
where your absence
sucks and pulses
like a heart

### UNABLE TO SLEEP AFTER MAKING LOVE
### I LISTEN TO THE AIRWAVES

The clock, a candle
burning the long seconds

The streetlight,
a century

A single star
in a window
when a lamp goes out

Everything is sleep
except our skin
which radios the holy
darkness

\*

In the next room,
a woman making love

We hear her throat-
songs like stones
falling underwater

A train blows the cool distance
Prairie moan, tunnel moan

Our blood wakes up
to come with her

\*

When it was still
summer I lay
in damp grass
by the woodpile

Heard a sound
of high wind
breath whining

Insect rhythm
rocking in the shadows
of the split wood

A sound so private
I had to touch
myself

## THINGS A WOMAN DOES WITH EMPTINESS

Sunday, the long tunnel.
I wake in the familiar weather
of your breath.
Your body gravity
pulls me in. Your house
pulls on my skin.
It wants me to grow huge
to fill the space of Sunday.
Unmade bed, bare rooms to mend.
An empty house will suck
a woman in.

I want to fill it
with my smells,
tomatoes boiled all day
to make a stew.
A house is hungry.
It will chew a woman
trained to fill the hunger in.
I give it my body,
my salt smell. I feed it
steamy laundry
hung in the slate-walled cellar,
dust, coffee,
smell of last night's love
like bleach on my fingers.

The church bells and the freeway
are an early hymn.
Sunday spreads like a hole
and I fall in the hollows of you.
I cringe from the needs
that translate into love
like bowls, beds. The rooms all stare.
I do all the things a woman does
with emptiness.

Fill the house with my clothes.
Fill my body with your child.
Fill all your holes with my loving
or bolt from this cave
in which I cannot find myself,
my own life
or any of my real names for being.

BLANCHE
*for my grandmother*


She's shrunk now and blue,
the color of smoke or a jelly glass.
We sit drinking Sanka.
"I'm a little fuzzy in the mornings," she says.
"I can't remember things.  I need lists:
what day the doctor, hairdresser Tuesday,
milk, aspirin, sherry.
Just two small glasses in the afternoon."

I talk because I'm afraid
to ask how are you,
afraid she'll say she can't remember
or tell me her back is burning.
Her eyes cloud some days so she thinks she's been crying
but can't remember why.
"You know, it's not so bad
here at the residence," she says.
"It's just dull."
Plants on sill in pink foil,
poinsettias still blooming in March,
the box room lined with photos of her husband
who died in 1946
and I wonder if she's been touched since
beneath the nylon layers,
powder and sag in the swell under her girdle
or if she ever liked it.

I say, "Let's get down the albums."
We sit side by side on the bed and turn over 80 years,
black pages, gray snow,
the silver her family never found in Colorado.
"Here we are posing," she says.
"This is so old, before the scarlet fever took my hair.
My mother was not a happy woman.

Here's Father, Ephraim, a depot master in Westcliff,
population about 40 and 10 of them were us.
We could ride the train free,
but Mother never went anywhere, just France once.
They shipped over all the mothers of the war dead.
She went to Don's grave.
He drowned in a ditch near Avignon
two days after Armistice.
Here she is again.
I always said I never wanted to be a fat old woman like her.
Here's a picnic.  Berry picking.
None of the boys came back from the war."

Blanche brushes my arm like a moth,
holds the seven books of descendents,
every name in mind:  Arthur, George, Bertha, Edith, Jim, Kate.
"Nell's dead now.  *I get fuzzy in the mornings.*"
Eighty years of dinners,
blades poised over the neck of the turkey,
fresh babies propped on women's knees.
Blur:  the speed at which Blanche and I fall
dizzy through the century of our births
grabbing fragments of all that is lost.
"Here is Italy!  Is it?  Is it Rome?  Is it Florence?
Where are my glasses?  It's all out of order.
Oh my poor brain."

She grows younger, moored to the stuck faces.
"Look, my queer wedding.
Your grandfather Paul on a train.
I guess it all did add up.
*So much happened.*"

Blanche leans back into pillows, her chest concave.
For no apparent reason, she remembers a tiny white coffin

in the parlor upstairs from the train depot
where she lived as a girl.
Perfumed flowers in the dust.
The baby's closed eyelids, blueveined,
lips translucent as insect wings and the hair—

"The hair," she says,
"I wanted to touch it just once.
It was golden.  No one was looking.
I stretched out one finger
but there was such a sadness in the house,
I felt I shouldn't touch it.
A sister.
And no one ever spoke of her again.
Imagine.
She could have had a whole life."

## LETTER TO A CHILD NOT BORN

Remembering days when I desired you
to fill the empty future,
a way outside of me
to give my life a name — *mother* —
the way a small town makes the map —
but now you're gone.
Before you ever got to grow a full spine
or split your cells into the face
that was spilling out of you.

Two days after the abortion,
you are absence, ache, a small bloodstream
sucked back to the other side of being born.
Gone, a season I slept through,
something missing that never was,
chance to make something up
out of just being alive.

Heart, old tree-knot.
Womb, empty in the love house.

How can I place my hands on a death
that no one calls a death?
I can't grieve for you in open sun
but hide you like a lie
I have lived for so long
I have become it.
You move alongside my life,
unnamed, *not, no,*
out of my body,
into the emptiness you inhabit.

Maybe one day I will feel you
at home in me again
caught in the hole
in my heart where my own death blows
its wind through an open door.

## We Were Raised on This Dream
### *for Jenné Andrews*


You hold the wedding dress a woman sewed
Press it to your body loving its shadow
*Heirloom lace*   You say   *Someday*

I think of the name at nineteen
I so willingly gave away
in exchange for the kitchen bed
where the juices cooked and stewed
and he came home to me,
mama, maker,
ready to eat my buttery thighs,
the stove hot hunger between my legs
Under my skin was my face peeling off
saying *Man I can't feed you*

You say *casserole,* you say *the way his tongue*
but what will you sell off
to pay for the hours you no longer have
signed in your own voice,
to pay for the silence as a hired killer
when it took so long to learn to love
that emptiness we live on
Say *blanket,* say *baking*
say *dying but when he touched me —*

And still I want that, too
Someone who doesn't disappear,
who stays deep in the daily years
The welling of music
only loving can train us to hear,
half knowing it will never stay with us
like loneliness

So we wake up wondering
why we don't get it
The fifty-years bed, china passed hand to hand
down all the family's mute and smiling women

*I'm saving it for your wedding,* says your mother
Polished silver, stained glass, cast iron
*You'll be settled*
You think of dust and arguments
You don't get it —
the table, the curtains,
the cradle, the name

You have your own
It's never enough and it's all we have —
our names and naming, that silence
when poetry is all we have left
and that seems so little
and so immense

## The Separation/Ancient History

Sometime after we found him face down drunk
on the living room floor, breakfast light steaming in
clean over his back from the picture window,
my mother threw my father out.
He stayed downtown at the Francis Drake Hotel,
close to the office. He'd come on weekends
to see my sister and me. Mother
would leave the house, tight-lipped.
Father brought presents: Valentine chocolates,
a paperweight for my mother. He showed us
the brass heart open in a velvet box.
I touched it cold and stone.

We went to the Shrine Circus to have fun,
watch the clowns climb out of a tight packed car
or was it merely to keep us staring
at the pink spotlight so the tightrope walker
could appear high in a sudden moment
near the starry ceiling of the auditorium.
I stopped believing in shadows and doves
the magician pulled from his loose black sleeves.

After the day in which we did not laugh,
we went back to the hotel, ate sandwiches
with plastic swords stuck through white bread.
Father drank black coffee, swirled the spoon.
No one said anything when the waitress asked,
*Where's the missus?*

When we asked to see his room, he took us
up the cigar-stuffy elevator, down dark floral halls
to the room that opened with a skeleton key.
Bed pulled down out of the wall and windows smoke-stained.
Newspapers stacked next to an old stuffed chair
that was empty. I remember looking past the room,
through it, to the definition of the skyline,

sharp and exact, black on winter gray,
to look away from holes in people
words were supposed to fill
and never did.

## NOTHING OF THE WORLD

Nothing of that early world
Not the summer voices of bees hung in fat leaves
Nothing of windows where I stared
at the luna moth, its luminous wings,
the eyes that never closed

Or the hush talk, Mother and Father
drinking while we slept,
late night jazz on the hi-fi
Sweet horns, boozey kisses
Not even the conch shell on the bookshelf
from their honeymoon to Cuba,
its pink mouth open and mute
but singing something ancient
I thought I knew the words to

Nothing of any of it
Dishwasher oceanic hum in the electric house
Backyards unbroken by fences
The field behind Foodtown
where we hid in high grass

Nothing would remain
and no one to enter the old stories:
Who was that boy in the woods by the river,
his hand under my striped shirt?

Why did my bedroom shadows bloom blue roses
in the bruised night?
Why Father finally came home off the bottle
and swept sad Mother up in a red shawl with gold fringe
They tried dancing the cha-cha again,
moved their bedroom to the paneled basement

Nothing could stop it
Not *Starlight, Starbright*
Not prayers
Not chanting the names of the neighborhoods:
Roseville, Shoreview, Arden Hills

It was over
They couldn't stop it
Ironing smell of humid cotton
I'd bury my face in the basket
Nothing would stay
My mother's voice, a wire across the wide dusk:
*Don't touch yourself*
*Don't think so much*
*Don't stay too long*

# The Funeral Home

I'd work there when the secretary was on pregnancy leave. Murphy's Funeral Home on Dixie Highway in the South End of Louisville. Jack's dad, flying to Miami in silk suits, owned the place. His brother once owned it with him, but went crazy in Korea, came back a pilot and dive-bombed the funeral home in a rented plane during his father's funeral.

Jack — Little Jack they called him because he was the son but weighed over 200 pounds — he'd go out at night and get bodies. He'd arrive at houses where a dead person was laid out in a bed, not usually covered, the family sitting silent on gold-flecked furniture drinking instant Maxwell House. He spent every day working around dead people. I'd have to enter the funeral home through the basement where the caskets were stored because I looked like a hippie.

Once there were too many bodies. It was Christmas. Everyone dies then when their families will hurt the most trying to be joyful. The bodies were lined up on metal stretchers out by the new coffins. I never saw death like that without make-up. An old woman was blue-gray slate and her eyes rolled back in her head, her body stiff and contorted the way they found her. When you die, the muscles contract, you make claw hands, open your mouth wide like a sigh or scream. Your spine twists back arc and your legs to into your chest like a fetus. You leave and all that's left is smell rot Krishna blue and then ashes.

Upstairs, I typed up death certificates and ordered flowers in the office. People would come in and cry to me. "She knew she was going to die," they'd say. "She looked out the upstairs window and said she saw Grandpa on a white horse. She said it was a vision and he was coming for her. We thought she was into the Jim Beam. Now she's gone." They'd feel better then. I'd listen and give them coffee.

I grew to hate gladiolas. And how Jack laughed too loud and too much because he was scared day after day. It wasn't so much the bodies as the live people that scared him. In the embalming room, they'd sit — Jack and Jim Ed and the dumb guy from the mountains. They'd hook the body up and suck out the blood and shoot in formaldehyde and it stunk like high school science class, burn your eyes. Jack and the boys would smoke dope, drink Coke, play tapes of Jimi Hendrix while the soul of the deceased hovered near as a pink fog in the basement before ascending to heaven to sit at the feet of Our Lord Jesus Christ. It was the living Jack hated because they were walking holes. There's nothing in your life so you fill it with people, family you love, hate and get tangled up with. Then they leave and you're left gaping, part of you missing the way you feel the space of a gone tooth with your tongue.

So Jack walked around scared in his Givenchy suit to make the factory workers from Chrysler and Brown & Williamson Tobacco feel small and country. They'd pay extravagant fees for cherry and brass caskets because they'd never loved enough and it was too late and money was the only way left to buy off the suck-hole they felt under the booze when the funeral was over.

## TOOTHPICK

There was the old woman laid out in her best dress, but her hair was matted and shoved all ratty to one side. The family brought snapshots to the funeral home to show the fat hairdresser, "Well, mostly she wore her hair like this here. Except a flip on the side. A course, this here was taken a few years back. 1967, I think."

Then the hairdresser would set to work down in the closet next to the embalming room with rollers, bobby pins, and hair spray to make her pretty again. Peaceful. Floating in boats of carnations, blankets of roses with a horseshoe that read MOTHER in gold metallic letters to drape over the coffin when it shut down black.

They'd come back before viewing time to check and cry all over again, drink whiskey from flasks. Warring sides of families from Virginia and Kentucky mountains stood on opposite sides of Chapel Number Five and smoked and glared.

One family didn't like how their Grandpa looked. They wrung their hankies.
"Waalll—he looks real nice, I think."
"No he don't."
"Looks like he's sleeping."
"No he don't, he looks like he's dead."
"He went to heaven with baby Jesus."
"No he just plain dog dead, you got to admit it, Hannah."
"He ain't dead."
"Is too."
"It don't look like him."
"What do you expect, he never laid down for a nap in his fancy suit, that's why."
"Gimme some of them sleeping pills doctor gave Grandma to calm her, will you?"
"He never even wore his fancy suit since he stopped going to church."
"It ain't that, it's the toothpick. He always had that ol toothpick in a corner of his mouth chewing, that's what."

"Well, let's go get us one, let's just go down Dixie Highway to Safeway, get us one of them picks and just stick it in there. Grandpa would a loved it."

OOOH, Aunt Hannah nearly faint, come in the office on the arms of big brother, collapse in the Naugahyde recliner while the cousins go down Dixie in the old Ford for toothpicks. So when the first whiney organ chords leaked out and the yellow-faced preacher began nasal *Dearly Beloved,* Grandpa floated happy at last on his final trail to empty heaven, chewing a tooth-pick in the Sunday suit he never wore.

## MOVING LIKE WIND

Passing the Islands of Juan de Fuca,
islands of rain whose name is made of wind
and sharp-leaved trees

How can you move like wind?
To grow your hair from the moment of birth
and use it as a yellow sail
toward your death?
Never to hold on to anything loved
but to let it pass through,
carrying you with it like smoke?

Move like the wind
by becoming empty
Let go of your name and all of its bargains
Empty your skin of touch, of hands
that pull at your thighs
Let go of your body
because it moves like water,
it moves like fire
but it never moves like wind

And how can I move like wind?
By studying curves,
sky that arcs convex over plains
Hours drying in heat,
whole afternoons of absence
curl up like the currents of wind

Wind and you disappear
You are no one
No one remembers you
though they pray to you when they breathe

Wind and you make love best
when you are dark and full of water

Wind and the silence of space
expanding into the feminine arms
of all the planet's leaves

Empty of yourself and forgotten
with a century's rain in your mouth,
move, you, wind,
listen —
the earth is breathing

## AT TOTAL ECLIPSE OF THE SUN

In this strange dark at noon,
through the false light of the world,
we see the dead, forgiven, float like dim fumes
from under the parked cars.

So they have been traveling
with us all this time—
Grandmother gone before I knew her
as anything but a soft row of buttons.
Gone on a Christmas, my father said.
The cherry light of the ambulance
blinked as her heart did not,
tree lights pulsing tinsel.
Grandfather fainted against the mirror
into his own reflection. I heard
his skull on silver glass.

John dove into heaven from the motorcycle
on a mountain blind curve.
Barb eaten too young by cancer,
her skin caved in.
Even the cat shrunk to bone in August dust,
breath stopped like an old fan.

The dead are with us.
They borrow the blue between trees.
And we never had to miss them,
only the smell of their clothes
was gone, only the hair
stuck in their combs.

One by one,
great clear birds of the wind,
they greet our hearts and empty streets,
our dishes in the sink. They bow
to our little hours made and counted by the light
that disappears.

Tenderly they remember our hunger
for sugar, our breasts, our open mouths.
Our leaves gone red blood back into water,
back into fire.
Back into dirt.

## JIM DYING

Jim's got a bad heart at 44.  I go visit him in the hospital
on Chicago Avenue, 3rd floor cardiac unit room 324.
He has plastic tubes stuck up his nose and looks pale yellow
floating fleshy in the bed.  It's winter,
there's a dried-up African violet next to the window.
I talk on like we're meeting for lunch at the Rainbow,
and nothing's wrong.  All the while there's Jim's death
at the black heart center of who he is,
the lover kiss you, eat you from the inside.

So Jim, we'll take a trip because you might die soon.
Take the train to Chicago.  You'll buy a Panama hat.
I'll make my old man drive us to the station in the Monte Carlo,
we'll sip white wine in the bar car, have lunch
with my uncle who works for Exxon, hear jazz every night.
You'll go down to the YMCA to get laid
by a young man who smokes too much,
come back to the hotel to tell me about it:
"He wanted me to give him money afterward
but that ain't my number."

Then we'll sit in the blue room smelling of dust
high over Chicago streets and I'll say, "Jim?
I want to sleep with you."  Not kiss or be sexual,
but sexual anyway, the way skin is,
naked against itself.  We lie together in kimonos,
watch TV, order eggs Benedict from room service.

Afterward, we just pretend to sleep.  Instead,
we each lie awake wanting to cry or take a picture of us
next to old floral curtains.  You're still young.
You say, "I remember being 29 like you.  You know,
I don't feel any different except I'm not so dumb.  It hurts
because you remember things at a distance and know for sure
they're over and you can't touch them again.
Like my mother in Indianapolis.  She'd leave every day for work
and lock me in the house.  She sewed for Jews.  I'd wait for her

to get off the bus, walk home to me with grocery bags.
Once she said, 'If you're a bad boy, I'll leave you.
I'll do just that, James Lee.' And now she probably will.
She's eighty and has shingles on her legs."

The room is dark and smells of stale smoke. Jim snores.
If he was straight, we'd have married long ago
and by now we'd probably hate each other.

## MONTHS OF THE AGING YEAR

### October

My grandmother's house
where she hasn't lived for years.
Smell of books.  A walk
to the rose gardens
where half the roses are dying,
the other half waiting.
It is old already,
the wind against the afternoon,
the conversation of all natural things
going back into the ground.
I ought to bury something
until the sleep is over.
Bury it inside myself
the way my grandmother
buries the present inside the past.

### November

Everyone hums the tune of distance
but no one remembers the words.
A blue light between our bodies
says everything.  We empty ourselves
of the moment
but it only makes us heavier.

### December

The leaves just found out they died.
They turn white, fall back up to the sky.
We celebrate by spending money.
We stand in the aisle of the discount store
making lists of those we have forgotten
to love.

And my grandmother remembers everything
of her girlhood in the mountains,

but can't recall the question
she just thought of —
*Am I old?*
*What day is it?*

December, white as her hair,
begins to snow.  The seasons
are older than we will ever be,
half of us dying,
the other half waiting.

And the old ones
who inhabit our death
peer out from behind my grandmother's eyes
for one last look through her life.
They watch us light the candles.
From inside the dark
they are moving their mouths to our songs.

## MOVEMENT OF PRAYER IN A CLOSED SPACE

In the belly of the church at evening
I sat under the angel windows

A great liquid sorrow
hung in the air, I smelled it

Faint blood light
shone through the windows
The light was not old
but the name for it
had lived and died so many times,
it spoke itself without sound
in the crimson and cobalt
angels' sleeves

I wanted to fly up to them
Over the coughing stillness
Over the prayers of the heavy coats
Up through the spiders
that spun shadows in the vaults

Wanted to rise up
out of my skin
naked as refracted light

Fly to the angel
locked in the darkening glass

## ONE SONG IN THE GARDEN OF WINTER

Our mouths steam
into each other's
I want you in the snow
through my clothes
before the white year
learns to speak

Whatever the moon
is saying
I can almost make
my mouth go around it

My nipples harden for you
under my sweater
Angels bend low
over the buildings,
hissing

One song,
one song only:
*Open me,*
*remember my hair*

In one breath
I kiss all the names
of the gods

## Zero at the Center

It was nothing, it was important
driving up from Jordan through hot bare trees
with a few heart-breaking flames of crimson,
gaudy, the light bent over backwards to please
in late October
I couldn't name it, knew I'd been circling it
all my life, this zeroing in on nothing important,
language playing with itself
Nothing!  Birds — name them:  swallows, starlings,
sparrows, one-body black cells,
scarf in the air,
a banner of wings and light
The red-faced farmers at the gas station,
their felt hats, their bellies

Begin with nothing like God
Try to erase your life attachments to bowls and hair,
hot jazz, soup (name it:  lentil, thin clear broth,
the elegant sky),
blankets, back seats, windows and saxophones
I'm trying to gather the messy light
up into something round, a mandala
3 o'clock in the afternoon
Nothing was ever so important to me
and I had to sing it like it would never come back
and even that didn't stop the light from going

## TEN-DAY FAST

The bells inside the birds
have something to do with the leaves
that breathe darkness
For days now this emptiness
spreads inside
the way water rings out from a dropped stone
become the shore
We arrive home in our lungs
Swell out of what surrounds us
Fat peony buds sprout on the red stem
Wash the body as if it were a child
Hands of water heal the breasts
Skeleton begins to remember
how it was in love
This emptiness at the base of the breath
knows it is alone
but forgets to be lonely
All the dark inside
gathers to tell
how we burst from the zero
How the beginning space that fired
through our first two cells
was the hollow
where love rushed in like a river
that was always there

## PRAYER FOR THE FETUS

Please slide out perfect,
my red tunnel waters baptize upon your head.
Please squeeze down the dark cave
between the isthmus bones.
Please in fetal heart tones
that echo out through Doptone amplifier
in the clinic office,
heart churning through placental sea.
Please soft skull bend,
please all ten fingers miraculous
and fingernails.  Please spidery veins
all over your eyelids.
Your lungs are filled with fluid.
Salty fish, make hands,
not fins.  Come out cooked up fine.
Yeast and butter rise.
Black eyes closed in the 9-month dark.
Rise little ass and clean intestines curled.
Lungs rise.  Crocus in a soil pot.
Water every day.  Put in just right light
by window but no floodstream beams.
Down on knee on low-down winter day,
pray blossom opens.  Please be
body and whole out there in mother heaven
on the end of your pulsing kite string.

## WOMAN IN YOU KNOWS

For women
a time has come when clocks
must be buried outside the city
Days must be renamed
We can no longer tell time
Time must tell itself
How can we hear its music
when our bodies are like streets during rush hour,
when words are hungry
as the pale light of winter?

For women
seasons are born out of our blood
The birth is constant
Now the summer moon is a slice of cantaloupe
over a silver lake
Now the moon is a red unicorn
hiding behind the trees
Now the moon harvests the darkness,
stores it in a secret place
close to the blood

Women know the cave fires that burn in our sleep
never go out
They feel the flames come swooping into kitchens,
street corners, shopping centers
Listen — you can hear the roaring
far under the earth
The ground is not solid
It trembles close to the tides,
a deep split sucking the cities down

And a woman
just before sunset,
her hands on the vegetables and the children,
her hands sewing the shredded day back up,
knows death moves beside her,
that birth erupts in her anyway

Women, the time has come
The moment is closing
like the door of the century
Wait—
it's opening

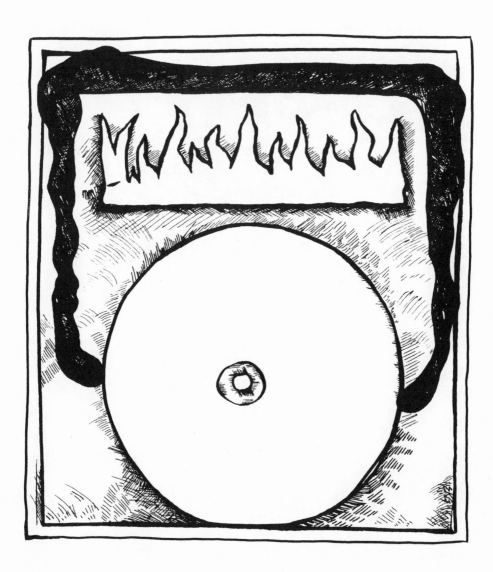

## III

ESTALEE

My mother-in-law says,
"What make you think you know
how to take care a black man?
What food he likes?  How he likes
his quiet time after working all night,
come home mornings, keep the kids off his back?"
and goes back to braiding Theresa Kay's
long Cherokee hair wavy down her small black back.

"And you tell me you don't know what marcelling is?"
She holds the iron comb in alcohol blue flame
till it singes hot, holds the comb to her hair
and pulls out the knotlocks.  "Now I don't want no
nappy-headed grandchildren."

At the crib Sundays, football on the fat color TV,
she cooks in the downstairs kitchen green tomatoes
Burt and I bring her from our garden two blocks away.
Slowly slice on blue Melmac plates, sprinkle out
white flour on two-foot strip of wax paper,
dip in egg and roll in flour.
Then fry in hot butter in battered Teflon pan
used every day to make dinner for nine children.

"What you daddy think about this thing you got?
He's a wealthy man, what he say about you
and a black man?  I don't mean to put you on the hot spot
but you ain't going to marry him,
now he don't make enough money for you."

Pan crackles, butter smack.  Across the street,
row houses.  Children hang off spindly trees,
play basketball on the old brick street.
"You never had chitlins either, did you?"
Theresa Kay plugs her nose,
"They stink *all* up the house on New Year's Day."
Estalee says, "Don't forget
where you come from, girl."

Tucker says his real name's T.Z.
"Down south Oklahoma, they call you letters
like Who Shot J.R.? So I'm T.Z.
My mother's Zellmore, fourteen children.
You young, you out the house.
Got to make room at the table.
None of this hanging round
getting your nose wiped by mama
waiting on you hand and foot.
Esta, she just don't know when to stop cooking.
Back in them old days we ate turnips.
All the time turnips, all winter turnips,
all summer bitter greens. Possums greasy like pork.
You hunt it at night like a rat, then cook it down
till it smoking. I slept in a car, no care,
no worry. We job out building fences with my daddy."

My mother-in-law dropped in at our house
and smelled the cat piss stink in the box
near piles of old newspapers on the back porch.
She grabbed Burt back in a room, said,
"Boy, now I didn't raise you to be no dirty nigger.
She ain't going to clean up around here,
you do it. You raised up good, boy,
you always had good clothes to wear to church.
She won't make you a good wife, she got a career.
Who's going to cook for you?"

"Oh yeah," says Tucker. "I want to be alive
to see my grandchildren."

"When you going to marry?" she asks.
"A couple bringing a child into the world
ought to make it good in front of God.
As long as you put God first, you pray,
you love each other, be true, that's the way
a life should be."

Dark sway of fetus in my four-month womb.
Burt says, "This close to nigger as you come,"
and we try out names by scolding
over roast chicken too pink. "Raphael *James,*
Anton *Lee,* Corona *Rae,* get over here,
now what I say, boy."

Burt floats in the bathtub daily
before he heads for the job, floats with Jesus,
the Bible's wilty tissue pages, water-rimmed prayers.
"You got to be satisfied *now* in your life.
You can't listen to no other folks' opinions
on how you should have this baby or raise the child.
If I want to have my boy circumcised,
it ain't nobody's business
saying it's going to ruin his aura for life.
I'm a strong man and I ain't had nothing
but a good beating
and they didn't call it child abuse then.
We got fed, clothed, kept warm,
taught to say Yes Ma'am,
pray on your bended knee
for the good blessing of your life."

Sunday. Late light filters the gauze curtains.
Estalee perched on piano bench looks funny at me.
"You know sometimes I get this
skeptical feeling about you.
Like you ain't for real.
I take it to the Father
and *He* tells me you ain't for real.
Now what I supposed to do about that?
I ain't saying you phoney just something tells me.
Like you work for the FBI or something.
You on a stake-out.
You always watching everything like you taking notes.
You writing it all down in some little notebook

with a scratchy pen.
I got nothing to hide —
you can look anywhere in this house.
It's just I don't know
what you doing in this life."

Dark star outside bedroom window.
He, a shadow, holds me and baby moves inside.
No moon, edge of his shoulder in black cold.
"But what did she mean by that —
I'm not for real," I ask him.

"You just got to remember," he says.
"She was raised to never trust no white folks.
She all the time be watching you, too."

BAPTISM

Miles Davis on the stereo and snow falling down between the buildings, he began to sing, *"How I got over / How I got over / Sometimes I look back and wonder / How I got over."* And *"There is a balm / In Gilead / That heals the sin sick so-oul / There is a balm / In Gilead / That makes the wounded whole,"* holding the notes out in a tremulous voice while I joined in on harmony, having learned the songs in junior high school choir singing all-white spirituals.

"Did I tell you I was the soloist in the youth choir when I was a kid?" he said. "Oh yeah. In my little blue suit and scared to death, humming in front of the choir while they rocking back and forth real slow in rhythm with the fans. First row was the deaconesses, the way they used to tuck their kleenex in the sleeve of their dress and fan themselves with the program? And out comes me singing, the choir goes huuuuuuummmmmm and holds it out long and I go, *'Jesus all right / Jesus all right'* and they echo, *'He's all right / He's all right.'* Then me: *'He's a doctor and a lawyer / He heal the sick and He feed the poor / When you strung out on dope / And you know you can't cope / When you ain't got a dime / And you doin some time / He'll be right there with you / And His angels too.'* YEAH," said Burt.

"Then there was the day I got baptized. You been baptized?" he said.
"When I was seven. At the Episcopal Church. My grandmother made my mother do it. I forced my mother to buy me an Easter hat."
"But did you get dunked all the way under?"
"No, they just stuck my face in a birdbath."
"Then you ain't been baptized," he said. "Sometime I'm going to do it to you."
"What are you, a minister or something?"
"A New Age Black Baptist Evolutionary Transcendental Minister from the Church of the Violet Ray," he grinned. "All my people been ministers, my grandfather, I got an uncle in L.A. — he used be a shark, man, running numbers, two-bit crook from

Tulsa. He had a hole drilled in his front tooth and a diamond inlaid. For real. One day he had a vision of the Holy Spirit, the diamond fell out and the tooth grew back till there was no hole. Ever since, he been a minister. And my other grandfather, Gerald. I never knew him but he pure-blooded Cherokee so you know he was into some medicine.

"But listen, here's what happened. They make you study the Bible for weeks till you know everything by heart and the day of the baptism they dress you in a white robe. You waiting out in the hallway with all the other children shivering and biting your nails because you know you going to get dunked in the white light of the Lord. They call your name. Out I go. The choir is humming, *'Take me to the water / To be baptized.'* The women is fanning and shouting 'Lord, Lord,' and they ask you, 'Do you know the names of the books of the Bible?' You shout out, 'GenesisExodusLeviticusNumbers, Deuteronomy-JoshuaJudgesRuth, FirstandSecondSamuels, FirstandSecond-Kings, FirstandSecondChronicals, EzraNehemiahEstherJob . . .' And 'Do you take Jesus Christ,' they say, 'For your Savior and your Lord?' You say, 'I do.' 'Then on the confession of your faith, my brother, I baptize you in the name of the Father and the Son and the Holy Ghost' and they hold your head and down you go in your suit and your white robe. You come up gasping, grasping for air, sucking breath and thinking you going to drown, your eyes bugging out like a frog and then it's done. The choir comes up huge, *'LOOOORD,'* they singing, *'LOOORD.'* They give you a Bible with your name on it like it was engraved in heaven. You run down to your mama crying, then run back to the changing room where the next child is looking at you like you just come back from the dead and it's his turn to survive and you know you done been changed. You know you new life."

His words hung in the cold air. "No," I whispered. "We never had anything like that."

## NIGHT SHIFT

He leaves the house, 11:20, winter nights
the cold howls in.  Takes the bus downtown
in thin leather jacket.  Ten years he's
sliced rubber, mixed adhesive, cut sandpaper,
hauled crates onto trucks near dawn
on the loading docks.

When he gets there, there's always some action.
Ray drives up in a '79 lemon yellow El Dorado,
he lives at home with his mama.  He and Burt
go out back behind the boxes and smoke dope.
Clarence Day jacks off between set-ups
in the spray room.  The foreman props his feet
on the desk by the file cabinets and snores
while the night drones loud out on the floor.

At machine number four, Henley's in love with Beverly.
She paces around in jeans pulled up tight in her crotch
while Henley drools.  Richie found them almost fucking
in the stairwell, Beverly arched back on cement steps
clenching the iron rail.  Dr. Doom, 275 pounds,
tells Burt the world's going to end tomorrow.
*Did you hear tap water causes cancer?*

Selma's worked the night shift seventeen years.
She and her husband live on a farm out by the river,
grow apples, tomatoes, fat rows of corn.
Day of her retirement, she tells Burt,
"I just never could sleep at night.  Took little naps
now and then.  Days I'm out in the field
smelling the hot dirt."

"Everybody on the East Side is sound asleep," says Burt.
"Stuck in 1965, cigarette pack rolled in t-shirt sleeve,
greased-back hair.  Sometimes I wonder what the hell
I'm doing in there!  I look around me and I'm crazy
in my sunglasses and my pierced ear.  Zuckerman told me
I was gay if I had my ear pierced on the left side.
I told him, 'Yeah, I'm happy.'

"But some nights, I just die in there around 3:30
thinking about you home alone in bed
while the mill heats that shit rubber up to melting.
I think about your belly swelled up with the kid
and your nipples and the little fuzz hairs
all over your skin.  I get a hard-on
back behind the machine and go get a drink of water.
The windows are all cracked out and the heat's no good.
Last night it was snowing in there.  I looked up
and saw all those stars just blowing in from black space,
coming in the broken hole I wanted to fly out of."

## Possible Love, Possible Sky

Some nights the earth seems possible,
something has returned to love us
All spring the hands of trees
make up green out of nothing
but earth and sky
I look back from my death
and say it is good
to touch you this way

Last night in our sleep
it seemed we made love
hard and quick without waking,
dove into each other
like the dragonflies' aerial mating swoops
that stitch the wind
We tore the heat
that lay huge on the darkness
as if two spirits long away from skin
took us in sleep,
remembering how it was to be born,
to return from those dark roots of longing
They envy our world,
this door between being and the possible sky
They long in their silence
beyond the black grass
to touch something living,
your hand, my thigh,
something that is made to die

On this lucent rain-dome night,
all that I fear giving away
returns me to what we are,
woman and man in this difficult time
Touch is the landscape
of what is possible

We make ourselves up as we go,
making love up as we dream,
and wake to touch what we've made

THE COMMUNITY

Hundreds of Hmong tribespeople have come flying into my neighborhood, deposited by the war in Southeast Asia. At the projects, there's trouble with the blacks. Not enough welfare to go around and it should all go to Americans. Meanwhile, white boys from the East side whose fathers work the 3M night shift with my husband drive over drunk in jacked-up pickups and write "White Power," draw swastikas on the project walls, then race over to Kentucky Fried, throw the spray paint cans in the garbage and eat.

Hmong women wrap their heads in long cloth that stands off their small faces like Nephratite. Wear plaid flannel shirts, long skirts, ski jackets. Strap babies to their backs with bolts of black cloth. If it's cold, an old wool blanket drapes around them.

On the first of the month, after welfare checks, the Red Owl aisles are crammed, Indian, white, Latino, black and Oriental, three, four generations of women chit birdlike at the produce, lifting grapefruits, abundance, bok choy, spinach and plastic bags into carts full of kids. An African woman in a long red dress stretched tight across her huge 10-month belly. No one fights over the food.

An old black woman stares at my husband in front of the frozen fish. "Ain't you a Hutchinson? Eddie Lamar? I could swear you Celia's boy, you favor him kindly. I know I seen you up at Temple Baptist." Burt nods, "I'm a Looney." "A Looney!" she caws. "Now ain't that something. $2.87 for a hunk of cod. Froze cod. Last week $2.53. I don't even *drive* a car. And I re*fuse* to turn *my* heat down. I'm going over to the butcher, get me some catfish. Nuf to make you want to go on a damn diet."

The CIA hired the Hmong to fight against the communists in Cambodia. Tribal people like Ojibway, no boundary makes them a country. Now after years in refugee camps, they come to Minnesota in December and hope their children learn English.

At the check-out counter, a Hmong grandmother in black sneakers opens her change purse, takes out dollar by dollar to add up to $8.53 for oranges, shrimp, lettuce, green pepper, 7-Up, and Mennon Aftershave. Looks up at the clerk each time as if to say *Is This Enough?* 12-year-old granddaughter finally pulls out coins, lays them down in a clean silver row till it all adds up.

Hmong squat at bus stops, lunch quick on fruit from a paper bag. At the school where I teach, a girl walked to the edge of the playground, pulled down her pants and peed. One boy wrote a poem about his grandfather who killed a tiger. The 3rd-grade Chicano girl wrote one about the toilet frozen at the project. Gertice Leon DuVal said he couldn't write nothin at all today because Donester Wallace, the new girl in beaded plaits, wouldn't *even* kiss him at lunch. Yeng, Yang, Vang, Kang, Kong, Blia, Dia and Nou sit straight at big desks writing words for things that we all know:

> Sun moon.
> My mother say what time it is?
> Snow fall like little rices.
> I have to go bathroom.
> You friend of me?
> When flower come roses all tied up.
> Red yellow yellow red.
> Goodbye.
> Hello.
> Hello.
> Two eyes and five fingers.
> Hello.
> Hungry me.

JOURNAL: JULY 16, 1981
    *for James L. White (1936 – 1981)*


In the last weeks, we didn't talk much.
That hot afternoon in the apartment
you made lemon chicken, I brought greens
from the garden and my newborn son.  I was still tired
from the birth and my breasts hurt full of milk.
You made coffee, leaned back in your chair.
"It's sweet for you now, isn't it,"
you said and I said yes.  You took your pills
in bright fluorescent colors, the utter blue
of the Elevil, the day grew hotter
and you were tired, too.  I drove you to the bank.
The car was in direct sun, black parking lot
baking the baby and he fussed.
Monday you died of the bad heart
that broke you for years.  I stood at your door
and rang and rang and the boy cried
in my arms, hungry for milk, hungry
for arms, you behind the door
in late afternoon heat, waiting to be found.

The last good night we had, we sat in the bedroom
with the air conditioner on and you asked
to hold the baby.  Then you read me from your journals
about dying while I rocked the boy to sleep.
There's no final sun or darkness enough
to know you're gone forever in the damp night.
July and the boats are still out on the water.
Curtains hang limp.  Today is your funeral
down in Indianapolis at Christ Church
where angels and gladiolas walk your skin
to sleep in the earth but
you're off somewhere else in a humid heaven.

Sitting by a window with coffee is the earth
and your skin graying, the earth.

The blank paper before your last poem, earth,
and the saxophone old jazz on the radio, earth
down here on ground where you've left us.
Music was earth and poems and food.
Old bed with lumps, earth, and now the sky
seems blue and large above the survivors,
as if we knew this was finally only a place,
not the world at all, just a place
we bring our bodies to and leave them
on a late morning feeling tired
of the old heart and its crazy singing.

IF THE WORLD IS RUNNING OUT

Let me still grow this fetus in my fat belly.
Let him be among the last to die.

In the spring when he's grown fully into his new body
I'll wrap him in a plaid pastel blanket the way
black women do in my neighborhood and cover
his dark face. We'll walk up along the freeway.
Papers are blown against the cyclone fence.
Lilacs high as trees explode next to the Evangelical Temple
across from the barbecue place.

On the bridge over the freeway, stop and look, child.
I want to show you this world. See how
we ride behind glass, hands clenched to wheels,
radio tuned to jazz to soothe
the cramped and hurried spine.

Here on the corner of 94 and Lexington three years back
is where your father was falsely arrested for aggravated robbery
because he looked like another black man in sunglasses.
Memory turns every pain to love. I still see
his hands on the Monte Carlo, legs spread,
gun at his temple, the angle of his wrists
in handcuffs as they pulled him to the car with the dogs
and he looked back, crying, "Call your father."

Your world, my son, slow St. Paul by the freeway.
At the corner, St. Peter Claver Catholic School
where black parents send their kids from Milton on down.
The rest go to Maxfield. You'll be bussed to Highland
with the Jews. Indians live up back behind the capital.

Earth, 1981. Reagan inaugurated as president,
peanut butter $2.89 a pound, the 439th day of captivity
for the hostages in Iran. Your father at the factory
cutting huge rolls of tape. He comes home smelling
of adhesive and glue in his nappy hair. Here is the SuperAmerica
where men call out, "Say baby, you in a fine and mellow mood today."
I raise my thumb.

Here's discount liquors and the giant grocery store
with boxes stacked to ceiling of all the things
we trade our time for in this life: toilet paper,
celery, milk and bread. Walk you down aisles
to say I want you to love the sad world. Love your father's
hands on the congas Saturday night full moon.
Love your mother's rice and poems cooking in the kitchen.

Love the mongrel dog in the alley and the seven birdbaths
kept clean by that shriveled woman, the one with immaculate roses.
Love the smell of barbecue Memorial Day, ten in the morning,
Cadillacs washed and shining in front of the projects.
Love the chipped jelly jar your father drinks beer from.

Love the dust on it all thrown up by the freeway.
And the green dome of the cathedral spectral in orange light
at end of day. Love your father on his knees nightly
in the pale dark. Love your own dark skin in this world
you sleep. Take all you need of breath and night to feed you.

## Don't Make Your Life Too Beautiful

Don't fix the three-foot hole in the plaster
over the stairway.
Don't sweep up the tiny specks of white
that gather in dust like stars.
Leave the hole under the fence
the dog dug in the marigolds
that never flowered.
You can look for hours at the pile
of shingles your neighbor ripped off his roof
and left to mold the green summer
with plenty of dark underneath for the beetles
and the worms to damp in.
Leave the rocks imbedded in odd places in the lawn.
And the black locust you cut down year after year—
you can let it become a tree after all,
towering thorns over the lilies and the peonies.
Look out the cracked window—
that broccoli just kept blooming
until the ice came down
and made us bend over our hands
in search of something we held and lost.
Leave it all exactly as it is.
There are heartaches enough to live for.
Leave the old worn boots stacked in the hall,
the rotten mattress in the flagstone basement.
Live out your ecstasy on earth
amid the flaking patio stones,
the boarded-up back door
and the rusty car.

Kate Green's first book of poems, *The Bell in the Silent Body,* was published by Minnesota Writers Publishing House in 1977. She holds an M.A. from Boston University's Creative Writing Program. She is the recipient of a Minnesota State Arts Board Grant, a 1983 Loft/McKnight Award, and a grant from the Bush Foundation. She has worked for many years with the Writers in the Schools Program, teaches writing at Hamline University and also works as a masseuse and Tarot reader. She has published poems and prose in magazines and anthologies such as *Ironwood, 25 Minnesota Poets* and *Ariadne's Thread, A Collection of Contemporary Women's Journals* (Harper and Row). Now living in St. Paul with her husband and two young children, she believes in "writing on demand. When the poem cries, feed it."